T0105663

Miracles Happen

STUART DUANE SWENOR

WESTBOW
P R E S S
A DIVISION OF THOMAS NELSON

WestBow Press books may be ordered through booksellers or by contacting:

WestBow Press
A Division of Thomas Nelson
1663 Liberty Drive
Bloomington, IN 47403
www.westbowpress.com
1-(866) 928-1240

ISBN: 978-1-4497-2548-8 (sc)

Library of Congress Control Number: 2011914938

Printed in the United States of America

WestBow Press rev. date: 09/27/2011

This book is written to the glory of the King of Kings, Jesus the Christ, the Author of Life who wants Christians to pick up the cross and follow Him. These are some of the miracles that I have seen in my lifetime. These same miracles can happen to you when you put your faith in Christ.

THE PROPHETIC WORD

So we have the prophetic word made more sure,
to which you do well to pay attention as to a lamp
shining in a dark place, until the day dawns and
the morning star arises in your hearts.

II Peter 1:19

The Ryrie Study Bible (New American Standard Bible)

I accepted Jesus and was baptized when I was about 16 years old. I believed in Him, but I didn't read the Bible or follow Him. I believe that God the Father talks to all of us. The question is: Do we respond to His voice? He talks

1

to our mind the same way Satan does, but God knows your heart just like He knew King David's heart.

When I was 21 years old I was in the Air Force. I was able to visit my parents at our home in Petoskey, Michigan, that summer the last two weeks in July. I had never been across the Mackinac Bridge, so they wanted to take me all the way to the Soo Locks on a Saturday afternoon. As we were heading toward Pellston Airport, I saw an airliner circling to land. I told my parents that my brother, who was in the Marines, was on that plane. My parents said that couldn't be possible since he wasn't due to come home until the following Wednesday. They weren't going to stop, but I said, "What if he is on that plane? Then he would have to hitch hike the 20 miles to home, and you locked up the house, so he wouldn't be able to get in." Since it would only take a few minutes to stop at the airport, they were willing. We parked the car and waited by the fence. We saw my brother in his marine uniform walking down the steps of the plane.

He saw me, and by the look on his face, I could tell he wondered how we knew that he would be there. I didn't understand it at the time, but years later a minister told me that it was the Holy Spirit who had spoken to me and told me that my brother was on that plane.

God talks to everybody. But how do we respond to His voice? I listened. He will speak again.

Destiny

'For I know the plans that I have for you,' declares
the Lord, 'plans for welfare and not for calamity to
give you a future and a hope.'

Jeremiah 29:11

Ryrie Study Bible (New American Standard Bible)

When I was in the Air Force I was on a plane with civilians
flying from Hawaii to Guam. We were not in the air too
long when the man sitting next to me and I noticed
a fluid flowing down the wing of the plane. Then the
pilot announced over the intercom that the plane would

be turning around and going back to Hawaii. There was nothing below us but the ocean. We went back to Hawaii and waited five hours while a repair was done before taking flight on the same plane to head to Guam. By now it was night. When we took our seats again we noticed that there was a spot light on the wing of the plane for the entire flight. This could have meant death in the ocean for all of us, but God spared each one of our lives that day. God preserved all of our lives for a reason. He has a plan for each one of us, and none of our plans were fulfilled yet.

ONLY BELIEVE

> If you confess with your mouth Jesus as Lord, and believe in your heart that God raised Him from the dead, you will be saved. For with the heart a person believes, resulting in righteousness, and with the mouth he confesses, resulting in salvation.
>
> Romans 10:9-10
>
> Ryrie Study Bible (New American Standard Bible)

In the summer of 1971 I was walking to work on a beautiful, sunny day. Yet I didn't feel like the sun was shining on me. I had a wife and three children, and still something was missing. I had a nice home, a good job, a wonderful family, a car, friends, and hobbies. Still, it wasn't enough. Later, I went off to be alone. I knelt down, I asked the Lord Jesus to forgive my sins, and I invited Him into my heart. I asked Jesus to be my Teacher. Then I began to read the gospel of John because in the book of John, Jesus teaches about the Holy Spirit that lives in the believer's heart. This was the beginning of my walk with Christ.

Overcoming Habits

God is faithful and will not allow you to be tempted

beyond what you are able; but with the temptation

will provide the way of escape also, that you may be

able to endure it.

I Corinthians 10:13

New American Standard Bible

In the 1970's I was working nights in a noisy factory. While at work on April 10, 1972 the day my youngest son was born, a voice spoke to me as if it were a person standing right in front of me and said, "Duane." (At that time I was known as Duane because my father was Stuart.)

"Yes, Lord," I said, realizing who was speaking to me.

Jesus said, "I want you to give up the habit of smoking so that my power can work through you."

I looked around expecting to see someone because the voice was so real, but no one else was around. I said, "Lord, I've tried everything, and I can't quit."

Jesus said, "Pray, and ask me to take the taste of tobacco from your lips."

So I asked the Lord to take away the taste of the tobacco from my lips. And He did. I was 34 years old, and at that time I didn't understand what power He was talking about. But I did understand the hold that tobacco had on me. I knew that smoking was a sin. I knew that every time I picked up a cigarette I was under Satan's power, and I was doing what he wanted me to do instead of what God wanted me to do. God knew that I believed Him, but what did my God see in me? I'm not a preacher, and I never went to college. I read the gospel of John first because it talks about the third person of the trinity, the Holy Spirit, which lives inside of me. I'm still a sinner, and I confess to that. But because of the Holy Spirit living inside me, I don't want to sin, and I can choose not to sin. Since that night at work I have never again picked up a cigarette. By God's power and grace I was delivered from that habit.

HEALING POWER

Let all that I am praise the Lord; may I never forget
the good things he does for me. He forgives all my
sins and heals all my diseases.

Psalm 103:2-3

New Living Translation

In the summer of that same year my oldest daughter,
Angel, who was almost 10, got a new pair of glasses. She
didn't like to wear glasses, and she said she wished she
didn't have to wear glasses. I asked her if she believed
that Jesus could heal her eyes, and she said she believed.

I called upon the Lord Jesus to heal my daughter's eyes. Then I told her to take off her glasses, and I asked her how well she could see. She told me she could see just fine, so I told her she didn't have to wear the glasses.

That night while I was at work, Satan tried to make me believe that perhaps Angel's eyes were not healed by causing me to think that she should see a doctor just to make sure. Satan speaks to the human mind just like God does. I said, "Get behind me, Satan."

A few months later, without my knowledge, a doctor went into the school to check the eyes of the students. Angel told me that her eyes had been checked, so I asked her what the doctor had said. She said the doctor had told her that her eyes were fine. Now, nearly 40 years later, Angel wears glasses to read.

GOD'S PROTECTION

Behold, I am with you and will keep you wherever

you go . . .

Genesis 28:15

In the 1970's I lived only about ½ mile from the factory at which I worked, and back then many people let their dogs roam free. At one time I had to be at the factory by 7 A.M., so I would often walk the short distance to work. One morning at around 6:45 as I was walking to work, three German shepherds came running toward me barking furiously. I simply put up my hand, palm toward them, and commanded, "Stop in the name of Jesus!" The three dogs turned around and walked away. Even animals obey Jesus. I believed, and I had no fear. To fear is to not trust Jesus.

I spoke in the name of the Lord Jesus, trusting and believing. There is power in the name of Jesus. Jesus said, "I am the Way, the Truth, and the Life." (John 14:6) He is the greatest power on earth.

MORE HEALING POWER

"I will give you back your health and heal your
wounds," says the Lord.

Jeremiah 30:17

New Living Translation

Sometime in the 1970's my dad was in the hospital.
There were two beds in this particular hospital room. I
was sitting in my dad's room with him, and the old man
in the bed next to him would moan in pain every now
and then. I watched as a priest came in and spoke a few

words over the moaning man. He rattled some beads, and then he left. The man continued to moan.

The Lord spoke to me saying, "Why don't you pray for that old man?"

"I don't know him, Lord," I argued.

I realized then that it didn't matter whether or not I knew the man personally, so I obeyed the Lord, and I went over to his bed. I asked him what his problem was. He told me that he was in severe pain, and the only thing the nurses gave him for pain was Tylenol. I asked him if he would allow me to pray for him, and he said yes. So I laid my hands upon him, and I called upon my Lord Jesus and said, "Please take the pain from this man in Jesus' name."

The next day when I went to visit my dad I noticed that this other man seemed to be more at peace. I asked the old man how he felt. He opened his eyes and got rather excited.

"What are you?" He asked, "A pastor or preacher? The pain is gone."

"No," I said, "I'm just a Christian."

He wanted me to come and visit him in his home town when he left the hospital. I never did. Now I realize my error. I should have followed up on this healing. I know now that the moment the Lord told me to pray over him he was going to be healed. That's not to say that God didn't hear the prayer of the priest because I don't know where his heart was at. Only God knows that.

God's Plan

For you formed my inward parts; You wove me in my mother's womb, I will give thanks to You, for I am fearfully and wonderfully made; wonderful are Your works, and my soul knows it very well. My frame was not hidden from You, when I was made in secret and skillfully wrought in the depths of the earth; Your eyes have seen my unformed substance; and in Your book were all written the days that were ordained for me, when as yet there was not one of them.

Psalm 139:13-15

Ryrie Study Bible (New American Standard Bible)

While at work I cut the palm of my hand very deep and found myself at the emergency room. I went into shock when I was laying on the hospital bed. My spirit left my body, and I was up near the ceiling of that room. I felt a peace I can't describe. I could hear the voices of the two doctors and the nurses as they tried to bring me back. I remember thinking, "I don't want to go back. I don't want to go back." My spirit went back into my body. My wife and four children needed me, and the Lord had other plans for me. I know now that He had more things that he wanted me to do, and he had more things that he wanted to show me. It just wasn't my time to die. I'm not afraid of death now. Fear is a sin, and worry is a sin. Fear and worry show that you don't trust Jesus, the author of life. As a Christian, these things shouldn't be a part of your life.

GOD CARES

Everything is possible for him who believes.

Mark 9:23

New International Version

I used to go biking around the Petoskey area. Just ½ mile south of my home was a crossroad linking the city to the country. The roller rink was on the corner. One day as I was heading out that way to ride my bike I saw a woman across from the roller rink walking around looking down. I stopped my bike and asked the woman if there was a problem. She said she had lost her car keys. I told her I would help her, and I began to look for the keys. Neither of us could find them. I said to the woman, "I know who knows where the keys are."

"Who?," she asked.

"Jesus," I said. "Let's pray to him. Lord, please help us to find the keys. In Jesus' name. Amen."

We began to look for the keys again, and we saw something shiny on the ground in front of us. It was the keys. Thanking Jesus, I picked up the keys, gave them to the woman, and resumed my bike ride. I never saw the woman again. But I believe this was one of those "divine appointments" set up by God himself for me to be used of him. God cares about even the small things in our lives. God cared about this woman finding her keys.

MUSTARD SEED FAITH

Jesus said, ". . . if you have faith the size of a mustard seed, you will say to this mountain, 'Move from here to there,' and it will move, and nothing will be impossible to you."

Matthew 17:20

Ryrie Study Bible (New American Standard Bible)

Some time that same summer I was golfing with my friend Gary at a golf course about 11 miles from my home in Petoskey. Gary, who is also a Chrisitan, lived in a town a few miles on the other side of the golf course.

We played the back nine holes because it was longer and more wide open. When we finished, we were walking up the hill to the parking lot, and Gary discovered that he had lost his keys. He decided to retrace his steps on the golf course to look for his keys, and if he couldn't find them he would call his wife and have her bring the other set of keys.

I went home and was eating my lunch when the Lord reminded me of the woman with the lost keys. I pushed my lunch aside and called the golf course to see if Gary was still there. He was. He came to the phone, and I asked him if he had found his keys. He hadn't found them. I said, "Gary, I know who knows where your keys are."

"Who?" he asked.

"Jesus," I said, "So let's pray and ask him to show you where the keys are."

We prayed over the phone, and I said, "Now go, and Jesus will find your keys for you. Call me back when you find them." After only about 10 minutes my phone rang. Gary had found his lost keys.

God talks to each one of His children. Do we respond to His voice in obedience? Do we trust Him?

JUST CALL ON JESUS

The righteous person faces many troubles, but the

Lord comes to rescue each time.

Psalm 34:19

New Living Translation

In 1981, the factory at which I worked went through some changes. Fortunately I still had a job there, but I wasn't making as much money, so to compensate for that loss I got a paper route delivering the "Super Shopper" on the weekends. My oldest daughter had graduated and left home, so there were still five of us. Three major blizzards passed through the upper Midwest and the Great Lakes during the winter of 1981-1982. The storms came three weekends in a row. After each storm, by Monday morning the sun would shine. One of those storms was so bad highway 131 drifted shut and was closed south of Petoskey. One of those weekends, my wife and I loaded up the station wagon with the papers we were to deliver. My wife would drive and I would put the papers in the tubes next to the mailboxes. It was after 5pm, so it was getting dark. We were going up a hill that was icy, but we didn't realize just how icy it was. At one point the car wheels started spinning, so I got out to see if I could push the car from behind. After just a minute of futile pushing I thought that the car was going to go backwards down the hill, and my wife would certainly be injured. So with one more push I prayed, "Jesus, I need your help." The car suddenly went up the hill as if it were on bare pavement. I couldn't even run to catch up to it. I said, "Thank you, Jesus."

So, why me, Lord? Why do I see all these miracles? Why do I trust in Jesus? Where does this trust come from? And why don't other Christians see what I see? I don't see this kind of faith flowing in all Christians. Some people shy away from me when I share these stories. It's almost as if they are afraid of the power of God or they don't want to get too close to Him. It shouldn't be this way. We should run to God. He wants us to run to Him.

No Idols

Those who worship false gods turn their backs on
all God's mercies.

Jonah 2:8

New Living Translation

By 1982 my two girls had graduated and moved out of
the house, so I had my two boys left at home with my
wife and me. In the summer of 1985 I decided a small
car might be economical, so I began my search for Ford
Motor Company's EXP, which had come out in 1982. I
had heard that in 1986 Ford would be changing the body

of the model a bit, and I liked the body of the earlier model, so I prayed, asking God to show me where to find an older model EXP. I also knew that the newer model would be more expensive. I began looking in car swap books. I found one EXP and called the owner about it, but I didn't purchase it. Sometime later I bought another car swap book and saw an EXP with low mileage priced at $6200. I thought I had already called on this one, so I wasn't going to pursue it, but I heard the Lord say, "Are you sure you called on this one?" I felt that nudge, so I called the owner in Detroit. He said he had just listed this car in the Detroit paper for $5850. So I drove to Detroit and purchased the car at the lower price.

The God I worship already knew ahead of time the car that was the right purchase for me. This car would not become an idol to me because I believe it was a gift to me from the Father above. In the seven years that I owned it, it never even got a dent in it. So many Christians miss out on what God wants for them, and they don't even know it. Sometimes they discover this after the fact. On the other hand, some Christians are blessed in many ways, but they don't attribute it to God who gave them the blessing. We need to count our blessings and daily thank God, the One who gives the blessing.

GOD ANSWERS PRAYER

Again I say to you, that if two of you agree on earth
about anything that they may ask, it shall be done
for them by my Father who is in heaven.

Matthew 18:19

Ryrie Study Bible (New American Standard Bible)

On a Saturday morning in October of 1983, my daughter
Robin was traveling to Flint for the weekend to visit one
of her college friends. She called me to say that her car
had broken down. Apparently she was at a mechanic's
shop, but the mechanic said that he wouldn't be able

to fix the car until Monday. She was stuck in a small town all alone and had no place to go and no way to get there. I told her I would pray about the situation, and we hung up the phones. I asked the Lord Jesus to work in the mechanic's heart to be able to fix her car immediately. Fifteen minutes later Robin called me to say that the mechanic would be able to fix her car right then. I rejoiced with her and told her how I had prayed. In a few hours she was on her way to her destination.

This mechanic may never know how the Lord worked through him that day or that he was part of God's plan to get my daughter to her destination. God works in mysterious ways.

SAFETY AND PROTECTION

May the beloved of the Lord dwell in security by
him, who shields him all the day, and he dwells
between his shoulders.

Deuteronomy 33:12

Ryrie Study Bible (New American Standard Bible)

I needed a new winter hobby, so I decided to learn how
to downhill ski. On a Saturday in December in the late
1980's I was anxious to get to the ski hill, but I had to
do some plumbing work on my house before I could

leave. I had to make a quick run to a local store for some plumbing parts, and the Lord showed me His mercy and His grace upon returning to my house. My house is on the top of a hill, and the driveway is steep and along an embankment. In the winter this can be treacherous, so to make it up the driveway you have to drive on the wrong side of the road, aim the vehicle up the driveway, get a running start, and coast up at that perfect speed. On this particular day, I wasn't thinking about getting up the driveway; I was just focused on getting to the ski hill. So about three-fourths of the way up the driveway my car started spinning its wheels on ice. I started going backwards down the hill, and I knew I would go down over the embankment. Fear gripped my heart just for a moment, but I took control of my thoughts, and I prayed, "No! Stop the car, Jesus!" Immediately the car stopped moving. Fear quickly came again, and I wondered if I should get out of the car to be safe. Once again I took control of my thoughts. I realized that since the car had stopped I was safe. I opened my door and saw that the car had already begun to go over the embankment, but Jesus had protected me. I took a good look at the way the car was on the hill, got back in the car, turned the steering wheel, and was able to slowly back down the driveway. I'm sure that if I hadn't called out to Jesus, the car would have gone over the embankment.

God Preserves Us

God arms me with strength, and he makes my way

perfect.

Psalm 18:32

New Living Translation

One September night in the late 1980's I got a phone call from a young lady whom I had not seen in about four years. Years earlier I had told her that if she ever needed help that she could call me. She was now 17, and she was calling me with her troubles. As I sat at my kitchen bar table listening, I realized that I didn't want

to get involved, but God spoke to me, "Deny yourself."
I decided I needed to follow through with my words to
help this girl. She was out in the country, and I noticed
the road was freshly paved, so I was driving around 65
mph. I saw something tan in my peripheral vision, and
then I saw a deer standing about as high as my windshield
only about 6 to 10 feet in front of me. At that speed that
deer should have gone through my windshield and killed
me! But the deer never touched me or my car. I checked
the car in the day light the following day, and there wasn't
a scratch on it. I told a co-worker about this the next
day, and he agreed that at that speed and with the car's
aerodynamics I should be dead.

I have a book written by Billy Graham entitled
<u>Angels</u>. It explains how angels are God's secret agents.
Every true believer in Christ should be encouraged and
strengthened in knowing that angels are watching, and
they mark your path. They superintend the events of your
life and protect the interest of the Lord God. They are

always working to promote His plans and to bring about His highest will for you. Angels are interested spectators and mark all that you do. I Corinthians 4:9 says that we are made a spectacle to the world and to angels and to men. I am convinced that in this instance there was an angel protecting me.

GOD GIVEN GIFTS

And God has appointed in the church, first apostles,
second prophets, third teachers, then miracles, then
gifts of healing, helps, administrations, various
kinds of tongues.

I Corinthians 12:28

Ryrie Study Bible (New American Standard Bible)

Also in the late 1980's we had a young minister in the
church that we attended. He recognized the gifts flowing
in me. I was offered the position of elder in the church,
but I was not comfortable speaking in front of people.

This minister told me that if anybody was qualified to be an elder, I was. Although I was not comfortable speaking to a group of people, I was comfortable praying in front of people.

One evening I was asked to read a scripture. I opened to the book of Colossians and read what I felt the Lord had laid on my heart. Later, the minister told me that he was amazed that this was the very scripture he was using for the next Sunday's sermon.

On another Sunday evening this minister came to my house and shared with me that he and a friend were going to a healing service for a little baby who was very ill and had difficulty breathing. The doctors couldn't figure out the cause of the baby's illness. We went and laid hands on the baby. We called on the Lord Jesus to heal this baby, knowing that divine healing comes from the Lord Jesus. Jesus heard our prayers, and the baby recovered.

As Christians, we need to discover what our God given gifts and talents are, and we need to allow the Lord to use them in us so that others can be blessed.

Help In Time Of Need

Ask, and it will be given to you.

Matthew 7:7

In 1994 my wife and I decided to take a vacation and visit my son who was at an Air Force base in North Carolina. The day before we were to leave I was looking for my wallet because I wanted to go to the gas station to fill up my car in preparation for the trip. Both my wife and I searched the house for about an hour with no luck. I even called the golf course where I had golfed the day before to see if I had lost it there.

It wasn't there. Finally the Lord reminded me about the car keys that were lost, and I realized that I had not asked the Lord to help us find my wallet. So I sat in my recliner and prayed. I didn't realize until I sat down that I had become anxious and agitated. When I was relaxed a thought occurred to me, and I said, "That's odd. Why would my wallet be there?" I went into my bedroom. Above my closet was a plastic bag with some clothes in it. My wallet was on top of this bag. After thinking about it, I realized that after golfing the day before, I probably had my wallet in my hand because the pants that I had on didn't have any pockets. I remembered getting one of those bags down, and I must have laid my wallet up there without even realizing that I did.

I realized then that I can't question God's voice and his direction even if it sounds strange. I would never have thought to look up on my closet for my wallet. But because I prayed, God showed me. And I listened. I could have chosen to ignore the possibility that my wallet was up on my closet. Then I may not have found the wallet for years. All things are possible with Christ.

GOD'S FAITHFULNESS

Know therefore that the Lord your God, He is God,

the faithful God . . .

Deuteronomy 7:9

In the late 1990's we were on a vacation to see Stone Mountain. We were going over Gatlinburg Mountain, and my SUV overheated. The transmission had lost a lot of fluid, but I thought it was running okay. We made it to my friend's home in the southwest area of North Carolina where we planned to spend a few days. We took the SUV to a mechanic he knew. The mechanic didn't see any damage to the transmission. He made sure the fluids were all full. When we left, heading back to our home in Michigan, I decided to go toward Atlanta on I-75. Not long after getting on I-75, my SUV started acting up. I pulled off into a gas station to get gas. When I left the gas station my SUV would hardly move. I pulled off the road into a parking lot of a small office building and stopped the SUV. I leaned over my steering wheel and said, "I sure need your help, Lord." I started up the SUV, and slowly increased the speed to see how well it would go. We got up to about 50 mph, and I told my wife we might be okay. I decided to get back on I-75, and I kept going at around 60 mph. We made it to Lexington, Kentucky. The next day I drove all the way home to Petoskey. The next day was New Year's Day, and I took the SUV to my auto mechanic in Petoskey. When I got into his parking lot, the vehicle just stopped moving, so I left it there. Later the mechanic told me that the transmission looked like a molten piece of metal and this vehicle should not have been able to get us home. I told him I have a big God who brought us home from Atlanta, Georgia.

God is so faithful to His children. He showed my wife and me His faithfulness on this trip. I asked the Lord for His help. I just wanted to make it home, and He was faithful to take us home. I believe He alone kept my SUV going until we made it home.

GOD'S GOODNESS

And we know that God causes all things to work
together for good to those who love God, to those
who are called according to his purpose.

Romans 8:28

Ryrie Study Bible (New American Standard Bible)

During the first week of December in 1999 I suddenly
had double vision while at work around 7:30 pm. If I
looked to the left I could see clearly; if I looked anywhere
else I was seeing double. I went to the hospital and saw
an eye specialist. He ran all kinds of tests on me and

could not find anything wrong that would explain my double vision. I wasn't experiencing headaches either. The specialist told me to come back in a month. I knew then that this was simply an attack from the enemy, Satan, who wanted me to curse my God. But I trusted that when the time was right God would resolve this problem. In the meantime, I was still going to enjoy life; I was still going to ski. Often, on the ski slopes, I witness to strangers about the faithfulness of my God. In spite of double vision I could still ski as long as I was looking down and to the left.

On January 1, 2000, my friend and I decided to go skiing at Boyne Mountain. Thousands of people ski these slopes over the holidays, so it was very crowded. We were on the ski lift, and I was sitting in the middle. We were six or more feet above the ground with all that beautiful snow beneath us. Suddenly the front tip of my ski, hanging downward, caught on a pile of snow, and both my friend and I fell out of our chairs. I hit the snow on the right side of my head. It all happened so fast. My head hurt for only a moment. When I got up, I looked to the right, and realized I was no longer seeing double. My friend was just fine; he only bent a ski pole.

This was a day I would never forget. A day God chose to allow this to happen in order to heal me and break the curse of the enemy. This was a day when all things worked together for good.

GOD RESCUES US

Call upon me in the day of trouble; and I shall
rescue you, and you will honor me.

Psalm 50:15

Ryrie Study Bible (New American Standard Bible)

That same year I was headed to Boyne Highlands to
go skiing on a beautiful Sunday afternoon. There was
no snow on the straight paved road I was on, and it
was nice to have clear vision again. I saw a SUV coming
toward me on the other side of the road when suddenly
my SUV was in the wrong lane, and I was looking at

a head on collision! I had no fear; I was calm. I said, "I don't want to hurt this individual, Lord." Suddenly I was on the right side of the road again. I decided to slow down, but when I applied the brake, I slid. It was then that I realized I was driving on black ice. Black ice is a thin layer of ice on pavement that you can't see. I told my youngest daughter about this, and she told me, "Dad, you can't die until God wants you to die." There was a reason God didn't take me home yet. He still had plans for me.

This scripture verse says that two things will happen when you call on God when you are in trouble. First, God will rescue you. God promises to rescue you! He won't let you down. As a result of God's rescue, you will honor God. To honor God means to regard Him highly or to respect Him. If you're in a car accident, you would respect and highly regard the rescue worker who removes you from your car. If you're in a house fire, you would respect and highly regard the fireman who leads you out of the burning house. It's the same thing with God. God rescues us from our troubles. We need to honor Him when He does this for us.

Angels To Protect You

For he will give his angels charge concerning you,

to guard you in all your ways.

Psalm 91:11

Ryrie Study Bible (New American Standard Bible)

The snow was deep and heavy, so I thought it might be a good idea to remove some of it from my roof. I'm able to stand on the roof of the porch and scrape the snow from the rest of the roof. Without thinking, I put on my old, worn, smooth soled boots and a slippery winter coat. I put the ladder next to the eaves and climbed up. I made a pile of snow near the base of the porch roof to stand on. Then I slipped and tore my slick snow pants. My foot hit the ladder, and it fell to the ground. There I was laying on my back on the snow-covered roof of my porch with my feet up in the air and nothing to hang on to. It was an eight foot drop to the ground below. My first thought was, "If I fall and break my back, my skiing days are over." As I thought about my circumstances I realized that the chimney was about a foot away, so I reached out my foot and steadied myself. I was afraid to move another inch. I was afraid that if I hollered loudly I might move and fall, so I gently called out to my wife, who had great hearing. As I was laying there I remembered the guardian angel appointed to me by my God. I was comforted by that thought, and I knew my angel wouldn't let me fall. My wife heard me calling, and she came and put up the ladder. I was able to get down safely. I serve a fantastic God!

The Bible talks a lot about angels. Like humans, angels are created beings. Colossians 1:16 says that all things are created, visible and invisible. Angels are among the invisible. Psalm 91:11 says that God will give His angels charge over you to guard you in all your ways. I believe my guardian angel kept me on that roof until my wife put the ladder back up.

Divine Appointment

Do not fear, for I am with you; do not anxiously
look about you, for I am your God. I will strengthen
you, surely I will help you, surely I will uphold you
with my righteous right hand.

Psalm 41:10

Ryrie Study Bible (New American Standard Bible)

This next event was set up by God, and I didn't see it
coming. Yet, it was His plan for me. I lost my job in
2005 and was eased into retirement. I had to sign up for
unemployment, and while at the unemployment office I

noticed that they had free computer classes. Since I had nothing better to do, I went the following Tuesday to sign up for the class. There was a women sitting next to me in the lobby. She appeared to be in her thirties. An employee came in and talked with the woman about the church they both attended. Then the employee left. I turned to this woman sitting next to me and asked, "Are you a Christian?" She said she was, so I began to tell her some of the miraculous things that have happened to me in my lifetime. Then I told her these same miracles are available to all Christians who believe and do not doubt. I told her that fear, worry, and anxiety are not part of God's economy, but are brought on by our enemy, Satan. She admitted that fear and worry are a problem with her and asked me to pray for her and her teenage son. I told her that I would. I have a prayer list for each day, so I added her to it.

The next Tuesday I again went to this computer class in the morning. In came this same woman. She had actually been scheduled for the afternoon class, but the instructor asked her to come in to the morning class. She came over to me and told me that my prayers were working. Then she told me something that I had not realized. She said that she thought our meeting was ordained by God. She wanted me to pray for her for the rest of my life, and I committed to her that I would.

Prayer is a vital part of the Christian walk. What could possibly be so important in a Christian's life that they can't find time to pray for family members and others? Every day I pray for my children and their families. I have 13 grandchildren, and I pray for them every day.

God Hears Our Prayers

And everything you ask in prayer, believing, you

shall receive.

Matthew 21:22

Ryrie Study Bible (New American Standard Bible)

In the spring of 2007 my youngest son, Shawn, called me and asked me if I had been thinking of him that day. I reminded Shawn that I pray for him every day. That day I had asked God to protect Shawn. When Shawn called me, he told me that he should have been killed that day. He worked in a lumber yard at the time, and he was unstrapping a load of lumber from his truck at a customer's house. His back was facing the garage where the customer wanted him to unload the lumber. The garage door was open, and Shawn didn't know the customer was in his car wanting to back out of the garage. The customer didn't realize Shawn was there, and he stepped on the gas and hit Shawn's truck. Shawn should have been crushed, but all he got was a bruise.

I have told my children that I pray for them every day. I've told them that any time there is trouble or danger to call upon the name of Lord Jesus, and He will be there. I wonder where our kids would be if more born again Christians prayed for them. I wonder what changes could take place in their lives. It's difficult for us to pick up the cross and truly follow Christ, but when you do, it changes the way you think and the way you live.

GOD ANSWERS WHEN WE CALL ON HIM

Call upon me, and I will answer thee.

Jeremiah 33:3

On a cold winter day, Shawn had a loaded truck to deliver near a lake. He took a wrong turn and was on a road that ended at the lake. Because of all the snow and ice and hills and trees, he didn't realize that his truck was headed right for the lake. He said, "Help me, Lord!" With the weight of the truck and the snow and ice, he should have plunged into the lake. But when he cried out to Jesus, the truck stopped immediately, and he was able to back the truck up and get to the main road.

Once again, I had been praying for protection for my kids because of the snow and ice. God hears our prayers. He loves it when we talk to Him. It is so important to pray for those that we love.

ONLY BELIEVE

With God all things are possible.

Matthew 19:26

Ryrie Study Bible (New American Standard Bible)

In the winter of 2007 I started to jot down all the healing services I have been involved with. In March my closest uncle passed away, and his children wanted me to say a few words at his funeral. The pastor of his church was speaking at the funeral, and I was sitting in the third or fourth row behind my cousins and their children. God spoke to me and said, "Don't you remember?" I was stunned for a moment, and my mouth probably gaped open. I did remember! When the pastor gave the opportunity to share words with the family and friends, I went up and shared the memory the Lord gave to me.

It had occurred about 20 years earlier. My uncle was not well, and I asked him what the problem was. He said he had had a heart attack because he had some clogged arteries. Immediately I laid my hands on him and prayed that the Lord Jesus would heal him. I felt the power of God flow through me to my uncle as I laid hands on him. I knew he was healed before I said, "In Jesus name. Amen." This was Maundy Thursday, the Thursday before Easter, and I was on my way to church for a communion celebration. The next day, Friday, I went to see my uncle and asked him how he was doing. He said that all of his symptoms had disappeared. I praised the Lord!

My uncle lived to be in his 90's. Now I was at his funeral remembering this event. God is so faithful to His children. God does speak to people. Anything is possible if only you believe.

GOD CARES ABOUT THE LITTLE THINGS

Whatever you ask in my name, that will I do, so

that the Father may be glorified in the Son.

John 14:13

Ryrie Study Bible (New American Standard Bible)

One of my hobbies is to grow roses. In 2007 I wanted a
yellow rose in my garden, so sometime in May I bought
a yellow rose and planted it among the rest. I had had my
garden for a few years, so I knew how to plant and when
to water and fertilize. After a month this particular rose

plant had no shoots and wasn't producing. I was ready to pull it out of the ground and return it to the florist. It occurred to me that if I can lay hands on people and they can be healed, perhaps I could lay my hands on this rose plant and it would produce. I did what to some people may seem odd. I got down on my hands and knees in my rose garden, and I laid my hands on this rose plant. I told the Lord how I had wanted yellow roses and asked Him to produce roses on this plant. Two days later I noticed shoots on the plant. There weren't just two or three as there usually would be; there were ten! God cares even about the little things in our lives.

If you allow the Holy Spirit to live in you, He is a living flame. Many Christians don't know this. Some people wouldn't "bother" Jesus over something they think might be petty to Him, but the Jesus I worship loves to be "bothered" about things. Some people don't want Jesus unless they're sick—they don't need Jesus unless they're sick. How was I to know 35 years ago when the Lord

Jesus told me to give up something that His power could work through me, and I would see all the miracles that I've seen? Now I know the greatest power on this earth is the power of God working through the Holy Spirit.

CALL UPON GOD

Call to me and I will answer you, and I will tell you

great and mighty things which you do not know.

Jeremiah 33:3

Ryrie Study Bible (New American Standard Bible)

On Easter Sunday 2011 while I was in church worshiping,
the Lord gently reminded me of an experience I had just
had in the winter. I had awakened one morning with a
sharp pain in my stomach area. It was so sharp that I
wanted to cry out. I remembered tossing and turning,

but the pain wouldn't leave. Finally, I cried out, "Stop this pain, Jesus." And immediately the pain left.

Call upon Jesus in your time of need, and He will answer you. He is faithful to His children.

A WORD FROM THE AUTHOR:

This book is primarily written to the Christians sitting in the pews. The riches that I have are not money or material things. The riches that I have you can't buy. The riches that I have are free gifts given by Jesus if you really want them.

Too many Christians are spiritually blind and don't even know it. They would rather believe lies and deception than know the truth. They support such people. I have decided to follow the Truth instead. My prayer is that you will, too.

II Timothy 3:5 says that people hold to a form of godliness (religion), but they deny its real power (the Holy Spirit). If you have received Christ as Savior, you have the power of the Holy Spirit living within you. It is a gift of God. But if you deny the Spirit the ability to work in you, you are sinning against the Spirit, and you will be held accountable.